QUINTESSENCE OF EXISTENCE

EXISTENCE

Ignored thoughts framed in poetic verses

Amitra Shankar Palit

BookLeaf
Publishing

India | USA | UK

Made with ❤ on the BookLeaf Publishing Platform
www.bookleafpub.in
www.bookleafpub.com

Dedication

To the ones whose inner minds are constantly in motion. To those who often have the quest of looking into things differently rather than ignoring things just as a mere thought. To everyone who look beyond the imaginable, distant from the mumpsimus theories. These stories from mind and life are penned down in poetic ways for you all.

Preface

Our mind is so much occupied with so many things. Some are deleted, some are stored while some keep floating unnecessarily even after being rejected. In literal terms, mind is the intangible abstract theory composed of thoughts, emotions and experiences. There is no classification like good or bad, important or unimportant. Few of my thoughts, experiences and imaginations are depicted in the form of poetry. Poetry has different forms and each story needs to be told differently. Those who can relate might have the same way of looking into things as I do. For others, it should be a soulful journey of tales from times and times to come.

Acknowledgements

Life does not come with a manual; it comes with a mom. As rightly mentioned by Martha Brook, the first acknowledgement is always due to my late mother who always saw the young, dynamic and budding writer in me. You must be proud now Maa.

To my beloved wife Madhu for motivating me throughout the thick and thins of life and pursuing writing. Not the least for gifting me my most precious Yashasvi, our five-month-old son. I always wanted that there should be something that should prevail even when my physical existence won't be there and something that he should cherish or boast about in times to come.

To Bookleaf publishing for driving this enormous force of motivation and technicalities for hidden and overshadowed poets like me. Without their inspiration and assistance this wouldn't have been possible.

For the admirers of nature, flag bearers of reality, Story tellers of emotion, Gen-Z's of Techno Genre, Lovers of Ray- Tagore-Frost and many more.

Foremost the due acknowledgement is always pending to

YOU. Your love for the subject and enthusiasm always provokes me and makes my heart skip a beat.

1. AI SCHOOL: THE INFINITE VERSION

I can see a distant lycée
Not so yonder, fairly a mile.
Rustling noises of pupils and preachers,
Echoed once upon a time.

The monument I see
Was not the one it used to be.
No windows to enjoy the fledgling of the warbler...
Protruding vents or outlets of ACs.

Once a library of timeless tales
Courtship of rainbow dyed imago's.
Once a mate with plentiful luncheon.
Whispers of fables ready for the show.

The birds I see resembled drones
Taking firm care of the property
Electric watchdogs and shining panels
As I come close to the "Luminosity".

The door I stepped on everyday
Had a radiant smile on a tilted moustache.
Songs of March and Cold December
Drops of ice , in asbestos did crash.

The locked and stern iron gate
Showed me the face of reality
But once I pressed the genes I do,
Word that poured was "Technology".

Once a while, the naughty ones
Bunk and hop on homely trees
Winds of wonder, heavenly and sombre,
Mind guided by a "source of carefree".

Beeping machines shook me up apart
As tronic voices shouted over and out
Slim edge tabs and zooming lenses
Ear-phone-faces did stream and pout.

Stories of Martyrs and lullabies of morality..
Exchange of ideas used to recur..
Treachery side guarded by goal and wisdom
Once a life, not worthy of suffer.

Pro active knowledge and surrender to time
Face to face they never see
All I'm trapped in hard core metal
Digital eyes burn and plead.

The place I resided, taught me well and long,
So 'literate' it pushed on me..
That I proclaim to develop at will,
In this progressive society.

I never dreamt of , never imagined..
Peerlessness and solidarity
Amidst the wonders I created in lonely past..
Shall dive into the artificially intelligent future in variety.

2. THE UNWANTED RESSURECTION: THE ETERNAL WAIT..

Chapter 1- The Everlasting Quest

" Hey Keshava..
Why does it become so necessary!!
For the mind; then without fear and worry,
Emancipated once from the 'despair and cringe' story".

"Hey Harborer of Humanity!!
Benevolent preserver of the Kingdom.
How does one captivate thoughts in motion ...?
Overpower theories beyond random and quantum".

"Hey Conserver of Omniscience!!
I, antecedently, already and still;
Still bestowing glory and glee until...
Absentee in impure minds; souls that thrill".

I; engraved, campaigned in 'Noble'...
Stout and sterile in young minds.
I'm alive in every mood that propels,
Pure and maintained in valiant-kind.

"Hey Srinivasa...
Why does the exertion still haunt ?
Or the works that remain worthy to flaunt,
Prickles the sores right in front".

"Hey Almighty of the cosmos !!
Why is it that sufferings still echo..?
The boulevard rooted to thee,
Beside me; I find not my own shadow".

"Hey curator of Morality and Mankind!!
How on earth, do I need to set back !
How can a 'be-littled' soul again be pricked and sacked !?
How can he again miss the last sip and snack!? ".

I am there humbled and still.
In those who worship heart and soul.
I reside beyond wisdom and pupils;
Ignited in kinship and in love do I stroll.

Chapter 2- The Prevailing Rejoinder

"Beloved Bhanu Singh Thakur..!!
It is 'I', thy reason for creation,
My cosmic renewal and intervention,
The omnipotence; thy reason for dissolution".

"It is upon my eternal existence...
Your shadow reflects on immortality.
The path you chose and followed with perseverance ,
Should not ponder over my will depicting fragility".

"Emittance of bloom, glowing gold in shine.
That left the mortals unaltered.
Sprouting heaps of praise; songs divine.
Work left undone, devoured and tampered".

" It is me who decides, ponders, creates and takes away!!
And set the rules for the games to play.
Moksha that you have proclaimed with blood and pain.
With longing and belongingness
'Samsara' again you part of and will be..
For I am the one who dissolutes
And I am the one who creates".

Chapter 3- The Eternal Wait

Time bound eternity and the ever-longing wait...

Until a new chapter begins again.
And the whole Kingdom guards the gate..
Few negotiations to safeguard and make the 'sol' erase
the pain!! .

3

. THE ROAD I SHOULD HAVE TAKEN

Déjà vu!! As if time has travelled
Similar junction, two score years ahead..
This time no beauty but mystery unparalleled.
Dilemma struck night, horribly imaginable.
Twinning crooked lanes, both in abrupt shape.

Weary and soggy troubled feet
Trembling in fright, troubled in imperfection;
Destination unknown yet choice in need.
Timeless theories for a timely reach.
Mile or two less can be the glory lining to the station.

The lane at left with dents and cracks,
Had broken wheels waiting with feeble legs.
Turmoil so curvy with frozen backs;
Hunger so frequent with barren lodging shacks!!
Trust was the only payment; Hope must be the rent.

The right bent lane had steady commotion,
Running boots in hues and cries.
Racing minds ignited in delusion!!
Competency and hunger to slog the erosion.
Stop and go and go and stop, certainly as time flies.

The inner self did provoke.
The race called life has ticked off and started.
"Time's the key "my conscious spoke.
Into the wheels of fire, deviating right I rode.
Reached my end point, agile and parted.

The road I should have taken
I already took and managed time.
But the lonesome journey had already shaken..
The inner being longing to be taken...
Eager to hear, whispers sublime.

4. AFTER"WAR"D
AFTERMATH

I may have survived but a part of me died...
As I saw children passing by in remorse,
Emptied coaching bags and hunger on the go,
Dilemma struck eyes in "scammed literacy sorrow".
On the edge of their childhood, I cried.

I may have survived but a part of me died...
When I found skinny "good-for-nothing" men,
With stories of grief and stale bread.
Marching forward with grief and endless wait.
On the tip of their rifles, I call forth the bloody sight.

I may have survived but a part of me died..
When I saw her in the shadows.
Clutched to her knees, begging in sorrow.
In a place where none entered or should tomorrow.
I saw her hide in agony and "shattered pride".

I may have survived but a part of me died...
When I heard the sirens of turmoil chanting in the air,
Tremors on terrains overpoured in fear..
Gigantic geopolitics in despair.
Burnt houses and ruptured parks, once a cinematic sight.

I may have survived but a part of me died...
For now I feel the tiring soul of mine,
Amidst the intense battle of greed; intense and prime.
Done and dusted mother; wrapped babies in headlines
Life only worth surviving- this day again I pondered
over again and cried.

5. TENDER ROOKIE LOVE

We rode through the roads, as the helmets bang;
Busy streets, narrow lanes, noisy bridges.
Like rippling water, time flows into months and years,
And we shut out the world behind us.
Giant wheel of emotions, pile up tears—
Spin the reckless heartbeat,
I listen to yours in silence.
It's like the music I've never heard, danced to.
The rhythm, the groove and the ticker starts pounding.
I hold your hand as the ocean roars,
Wild mystic and astounding.
Presses its head against the sands' nest.
I find peace in commotion, failure and attempt.
Synchronising was never my art.
Rookie amateur love is not a new chapter.
It's the ink itself, writing us in places
we never thought words could reach.
With every curve, every turn, we chase the sun's glow,
Whispers of wind carry secrets, soft and low.
The sky blushes crimson, as dusk begins to weave,

In this canvas of twilight, our hearts softly believe.
You're a compass in chaos, a tether to the ground,
In the echo of moments, our dreams intertwound.
We sketch our tomorrow with hope in the dark,
Two wandering souls igniting a spark.

6. EPITAPH OF THE OBSTINATE- "WHERE CORRUPTION BREEDS AND VIRTUE SUFFOCATES..."

Here rests the profession that claimed dominion,
that draped itself in the rhetoric of leadership
and proclaimed itself the steward of tomorrow.
Rehearsing old quarrels upon a stage
whose scenery had already changed,
its script brittle, its voice hollow.

Meanwhile the farmer embraced the plough of iron,
the curing hands mastered the art of science,
the "modern educator" stretched knowledge beyond

walls,
the merchant trafficked in currents unseen.
Each bent to time, altering its course,
and the world was carried forward, so was the moving
mankind.

Its actors still deliver the same monologues,
shouting louder to hide the cracks in the set.
The audience grows older,
but the play never does, yet always in talk.
The costumes flickered in black and white,
at times laid at burnt cabins itself.

Here rests the profession that claimed supremacy,
that draped itself in praiseworthy of leadership.
and proclaimed itself the steward of tomorrow.
Hunger driven eyes; crooked souls.
Flabbergasting personalities with ideologies of own
The one rocking the cradle and ruling the world.

So let this stone bear witness:
every craft helped fashion the future,
save one.
The trade of power endured—

not as guide,
It really never did.

7. IF THE MUTED HAD A VOICE

Once a personified poet condemned; for he-
Chronicler of conscience.
the flag-bearer of silence of the wild.
Manifests on compassion and dignity,
Yet feasting upon when overlooked.
Euphemism polished by hypocrisy.

The hippodrome had sold all the tickets,
with a "bazaar" full of commodities.
Ready to be displayed before a cackling multitude.
Chained in infinity, pawned for a spectacle
They call it civilization, they call it entertainment
Misplaced mortals clapped and cheered in the tamed
music.

The mooing machine continues to record books,
Saddened in her confined enclosure-
Within her tranquil eyes lingers an ancient
reminiscence--

Of the hustling of the leaves,
Winds unsupervised and unbartered meadows.
She continues to provide nutrition.

The silent custodians or rather vanguards,
Within the selfless legs that move on streets.
Asking for none, comfort for once
Only not for the kicks and aches.
Drowned in pain and poison.
Demeanour, hides the pain within.

The rural timepiece, the roosting alarm clock,
Involuntary clerk in man's kingdom.
Enterprise of so-called divinity and punctuality.
Cut, cracked and cooked for feasts.
Bloody filaments on floor, left done undone.
Cooked and baked in joyous days to come ahead.

Then the one used in verbal spats,
the dweller in the drains, the common one in abuses.
Also minced for the purpose same.
Then the one, in the way to the shrine.
Unperturbed in landslides.
Imposed courier service in the way to heaven.

Not all but a few, sobbing bards do appear.

Slaughtered in a "stand still" mode,
Fanged and robbed of rays from spot.
Trying soul and hard with feeble feet.
On an impossible journey to the shimmering mirage.
Unknown of answers that lie in the sands of time.

8. PILGRIM OF ILLUSION

Beneath the sky's pewter grey
Amidst the hustling December epilogue
A child steps into the humming fair,
With eyes like lanterns wide and bright,
she climbs aboard with wind in her
hair,
Whispers of candy call her name.

Name unknown, at least not searched in the lustrous
event
Although the air is sweet with sugar and
flame.
The sun dips low in a golden
haze,
Old-school sounds from a boombox
blare,
As the fairground hums with the pulse of the days, she
looks amazed.
A distant whistle, the scent of cotton in the candied
version!!

Prancing painted pirouette pacers of wooden "cheer"

,

familiar like something lost, but never behind.
She passes the games, stuttering shots and the ring toss
stands
Time flies just in a blur of lights and
sound,
Gripping a prize in small, hopeful hands-

-

Like the memory of something she once pledge!!

As she fancies along, the popcorn's aroma
swirls,
The mirror wraps time, a dream to surpass

—

A jingle, a game, a call to play,
The carousel chants, her cardio knows its
song,
Where the rules didn't matter, just
yesterday.
She smiles at the girl that's there still.

Like sand through her fingers, or cracks in the lips.
The fairground's joy slowly begins to stir—

But then, a chill, deeper than the night,
The world around her starts to shimmer and blur,
Settles inside her chest, squeezing tight.
The colors, the laughter, the lights—they all scream.

The shoes on her feet—once new, now worn,
she tugs at her sleeves, at the verge of gait and
spin.
No one looks twice, not a second
glance,
Time slows. Her fingers, once twitching for life,now
numb.
She does not beg for more, won't plead for a chance—
But she knows the frosty streets are waiting again
tonight.

The chasing echoes of the Ferris
wheel.
Steps in, where the world feels strange

—

The man with a hot dog, an ice cream cone!!
more than just growling hunger, sanctity
restored.
Suddenly a fresh vibe, little density to her
bone.
Cheerleading from the sidelines, her heart pounced at
the thrill.

Emptied pockets with coins all spent,
Bruise of the past never built to last
She won't beg for more, won't plead for a chance

—

The fair's a fleeting world, a distant haze.
She learned to lean on the "tracks of unnecessary", built her own steps of dance.
A toughened heart, but a soul still blue.

Swiftly she feels gush of cold, distant shine of light bright gold.
Like the never-ending dream has come to an abrupt stop.
The world around her starts to shimmer and blur,
Settles inside her chest, squeezing tight. Numb and dropped.
"The last leaf" had already shed, removed, done and stirred.
Once again, another day of merry fair begins, as if none occurred.

9. ODE TO "SHUNDI" AND "HALLA"

The path that existed but never caught attention,
Paved uneven, yet greenery in borders.
Merry men, grazing colors unperturbed by any
distraction.
All owner of "peace and quiet", needless to listen to
orders.

Silently singing, dancing and showering vibrance
Syllables mute yet distinctively musical.
Hustling rivers of kaleidoscopic nature in abundance
Vivid nightingale sings whimsical

The other town had ruthless noise
All hail the king with pride!!
Silent echoes with murdered voices...
Chained with blood, trembling feet; hopes kept aside.

Dampened walls with metallic bar...
Corrugated iron and welding sparks

Treacherous blades with toxic taxes near and far.
The sun hurries here to make way for the ominous dark.

The sunny rabbits played here and there,
Monsoon months show a great promise.
Lantern lit drowsy nights; evening snacks to share
Not a single moment to miss.

Flowers bloomed and meadows free ...
Air filled with mystic fragrances.
Lotuses bright, smiled with glee.
Divinity resides with floral bursts, glooming occurrence.

The other town had stories of war, swords and pain.
Silenced for monopoly, helpless and wounded.
Tired and tested, palms that don't meet again.
The neighs of horses like never before, evil it sounded.

Two towns dwindling in a " twinship".
So near yet so far.
Shined in the times of ancient relationships.
Yet so reflective in modern scars.

Both the members now laugh in pride,
When they feel the countless repeat.
What has perished still lives on; never died.
All Glorified, cherished and Elite.

The devil also plays the rhyming game,
Slaughters are at ease with no mercy at any chance.
"Protest" is no word, not even in distant frames.
No time to visualize the nature, never ever by chance.

10. LAIKA

She doesn't mean that.
"No, no, no," she said. '
Little lemon pondering in streets of Moscow
Until "euthanized" for reentry back.
Nevermore.
As much as I say, "No night, the lamp is dirty."
she looked at me and said, "No, no, no. '
She dreamt of finger licking reality
trick or treating at infinite space.
Widow in the whirlwind
In the forest of flowers.
As much as I say, 'But this time I have to go.'
She stood at the door and said, "No, no, no. '

11. TO JAZZ AND YASHASVI

He came humming out of silence —
a half-bar rest, then boom—
a baby bassline wearing my tune.

Six months young, and already syncopated,
cooing like a trumpet in love with dawn.
His laugh?—
a snare tap, brushed with mischief.
His yawn?—
a lazy trombone sliding toward dreams.

He's me, remixed—
same eyes,
same grin,
same swagger,
only fresher, cleaner,
like vinyl spun for the first time.

I crash in rhythm, he wakes on cue—

midnight's his stage, not mine to view.
While I fade in sleep's soft haze,
he hums his solos in moonlit phrase.

Then, dawn comes cool and clear—
he sleeps like me, slow and sincere.
Mouth half open,
breath a sax's sigh,
and those weird little noises—
oh, the jazz in them could make angels cry.

And I think—
was I ever this new?
this blue, this pure, this offbeat?

He grins, drools,
drops another perfect chord.
The room shivers in applause.

Yeah.
Yashasvi.
My encore.
My jazz reborn.

12. SHUBHO DHRISTI- " THE SACRED FIRST FIGHT"

"স্বাধীনতা জিতল, প্রেম হারাল।
আধুনিক হৃদয় নিজেকেই ভালোবাসে।"
"Freedom won, love lost.
The modern heart loves only itself."
— From a Bengali Epistle on Modern Love

The conch-shell cried at dusk—shankha, pure and white,
A bride beneath the chandnatola, trembling in gold light.
Priests muttered mantras, flowers rained from trembling hands,
Incense curled like destiny, soft over saffron strands.

"Shubho Drishti"—their eyes met, bound in sacred glare,
The groom in silk, the bride adorned beyond compare.
Uncles counted envelopes, discreet yet known,
Money whispered under laughter's tone.
The sindoor stroke—vermilion and command—

A promise made, though printed, signed, and planned.

Banquet halls glowed with chandeliered grace,
Silver plates, gold spoons, a photographer's chase.
Drums of dhaak and perfume of marigold filled the air,
Yet beneath the festivity—calculations there.
A dowry veiled in designer gifts and cars,
Dreams sold beneath a ceiling of stars.

Then—honeymoon in Florence, selfie smiles in Rome,
She in chiffon by fountains, he scrolling on his phone.
Bills bloomed like tulips; champagne's foam and flight,
Their laughter rehearsed, rehearsed for the night.
Five-star silences slept between silk sheets,
Love replaced by paid retreats.

And soon, like candle smoke, affection waned,
Each learned success by what was gained.
She earned her rise, her city flat,
He dined alone, and was fine with that.
No fight, no storm, just a mutual fade,
Two lives apart, yet strangely unafraid.

The mangal sutra lies in a drawer, untouched,
The court stamps soft, their freedom much.
"Why cry?" she said, "I stand on my own."
"Same here," he smiled, "I was never alone."

Thus ends the tale where rituals bend—
A wedding that began divine, found a mortal end.

And "so-called love"—once fire, now traded for ease,
Replaced by comfort, careers, and peace.
They chose the self, not the vow once spoken,
For in modern hearts, the chain's a token.
The gods still bless, but quietly sigh—
For love now learns to live, not die.

13. SCAPEGOAT OF THE FOLK- A BALLAD OF UNHEARD TRUTHS

The tumbi hummed beneath a fickle sky,
His verses rose — too truthful to lie.
He sang of hearts, of hunger, of flame,
And the crowd cheered loud — but forgot his name.

"Takue Te Takua," a song half sin, half jest,
Unveiling what silence had long repressed.
He sang what they lived, yet dared not own,
The mirror he held cut close to the bone.

The stage became his altar, his creed,
Where truth was melody and taboo his seed.
Now polished voices repeat his strain,

Gold-wrapped echoes of his pain.
And still, he — the tumbi's fiercest chord —
Was sacrificed to please the board.

They called him crude, too wild, too free,
Yet danced to the same obscenity.
The ink that stained his calloused hand,
Writes now in softer, safer sand.

A storm of silence took him whole,
The singer fell — but not his soul.
For every note of longing sung today,
Still carries the weight of what he'd say.

They write of passion, fame, and sin,
And sell the songs he once wrote in skin.
Yet no shrine bears his humble name,
The scapegoat burns, the system stays the same.

"Sach di awaaz chhoti hundi ae,
Par goonjdi rehndi ae."
— Folk Saying
(The voice of truth may sound small, but it keeps
echoing.)

14. THE RETURN THAT NEVER WAS: REFLECTIONS FROM AN UNFINISHED JOURNEY

He crossed the border of memory,
not the one drawn on maps.
The mountains stood the same,
but their silence was different now —
as if they had swallowed laughter.

And in his mind,
Mini runs beside him again,
her anklets ringing like morning bells,
her chatter spilling like unmeasured joy.
She asks a hundred questions,
each one lighter than the next.
He remembers offering her almonds and figs,
her small hands cupping each like treasure.

The alleys were narrow now,
filled with echoes,
the scent of smoke and iron.
He asked no questions.
There was no one left
to answer them anyway.

He moved through crowds that pressed like waves,
faces blurring, voices colliding.
Every turn promised hope,
yet dissolved into shadows.
He called names that were no longer names,
searched doors that hid only emptiness,
and felt the city tighten around him —
as if the world itself conspired
to erase what he sought.
Even the raisins in his pouch seemed bitter now,
crumbled reminders of sweetness lost.

Once, Mini's small hand had held his finger —
so lightly,
as though trusting the whole world.
He remembers her questions
about his daughter,
and how every answer
became a prayer.
Sometimes she would sneak walnuts from his bag,

tasting them with a grin
that made the world seem infinite.

Sometimes,
a child's voice would rise from behind a wall,
and he would stop —
heart trembling like an old drum.
But it was never hers.
Only wind wearing familiar tones.

He walked past a fig tree,
its shadow stretched thin —
a remnant of home.
The door was gone.
The threshold still waited.

He sat beside it,
listening to time move.
Somewhere within him
a city of laughter stirred —
a girl's voice asking about raisins,
a hand too small to hold his world.

Now both cities —
the one he left,
and the one he found —
seemed strangers to his name.

Calcutta was a dream undone by guilt,
Kabul, a name spoken by ruins.

He could not cross either way.
The path back was barred
by a shadow called "past,"
and the path ahead
by a silence that had no face.
Even the almonds in his bag
felt like fragments of a life
he could no longer reach.

So, he stayed.
Between sky and soil,
between two vanished homes,
between forgiveness and memory —
a man who once sold almonds, raisins, figs, and walnuts,
now selling time
to an empty road.

15. BETWEEN FLAME AND SILENCE

Chapter I — Mātṛa-Tattva (The Essence of the Mother)

The morning smells of starch and soap,
the cracked blue mug of milk steams by the sill—
he ties his shoelace, crooked still,
and hums a tune from last night's radio.

"Ma, why do you never rest?" he asks,
his schoolbag yawning open like a small rebellion.
She smiles, stirring her tea slow—
"The sun doesn't rest either, son. It learns to glow,
even when clouds forget its name."

Then, as the kettle sighs, she asks,
"Tell me, what can a man do
that a woman can't?"

He blinks—
his young mind runs through a parade of things:

sports, shaving, maybe climbing trees,
changing bulbs, carrying bags,
funny things that tumble and flee—
until silence, clear as the morning glass,
fills the small kitchen.

He stares at her face, soft yet firm,
realizing—he has no answer.

She smiles, her eyes both teacher and prayer,
"Remember that silence, my child.
That's the beginning of knowing."

He nods—
his schoolbag heavier, yet lighter to bear.
She pats his head, her fingers thin as truth,
"Never think strength wears only a man's face.
Even the river, gentle as I,
cuts mountains into grace."

He runs out—
his slippers slapping puddles, a rhythm she knows—
and for a moment, the lane gleams
with equality, milk-white and warm.

Chapter II — Antya-Samskāra (The Final Rite)

The smoke curled skyward like half-forgotten hymns,
ash kissing the wind—
and between the chant of bells and the cawing of crows,
the Ganga flowed—calm, unjudging, infinite.

Two young boys sat cross-legged on the stone steps,
bare shoulders gleaming under the priest's low chant.
The razor moved—silver, solemn, inevitable—
removing strands of youth, one after another,
each falling like a fragment of memory.

Beside them,
their little sister stood still—her eyes wide,
her small hands folded tight against her chest,
as if holding back the sound of questions.

The priest muttered verses older than grief,
and the fire crackled like a language too ancient for
comfort.

A little farther away,
a man in a well-pressed shirt leaned against a column,
a cigarette dangling between tired fingers.
He watched the ritual in quiet absorption,
smoke curling upward, meeting the pyre's haze.

And somewhere in that mingled scent
of sandalwood, tobacco, and sorrow,
a memory stirred—
a morning long ago,
a cracked blue cup of milk,
his mother asking softly:
"Tell me, what can a man do that a woman can't?"

He smiled now,
a stagnant, almost tender smile,
as he watched the boys bow before the flames.
Their sister stood apart—her head unshaven,
her eyes carrying the same silence he once held.

He dropped the cigarette.
its ember hissed into the wet steps.
In that fleeting sound, he found the answer—
a cruel privilege, a sacred rule.

Only men shave to show respect.
Women grieve in silence.

He looked at the river, endless, forgiving,
and thought—perhaps she, too, keeps her head unshaven,
yet bears the world clean.

Chapter III — Tattva-Darsana (The Realization of Truth)

The evening sun bends low over the river,
turning everything into molten thought.
The man walks alone by the ghats,
the same steps, the same bells—
only quieter now.

Years have passed.
the smoke has long settled into memory,
and yet the question still drifts
between his heartbeats.

He sits where boys once wept,
where sisters once stood in silence,
and lights no cigarette this time—
only a lamp,
its flame soft, unwavering.

He whispers into the dusk:
"Ma, perhaps equality was never about the head,
but about the heart that bows."

The Ganga listens,
her ripples gold with forgiveness.
Somewhere, a conch sounds—
not of ritual,

but of return.

He closes his eyes—
and in that quiet,
he feels her truth flow again:
the mother,
the river,
the woman,
the eternal teacher.

16. THE WITHERED WING- A MODERN SEQUEL TO THE RAVEN

Once upon a midnight wandering, while I wandered, tired and pondering,
Through streets where smoke choked trees, rivers blackened in apathy,
While I stumbled, nearly weeping, suddenly came a flapping,
A shadow brushing against the air—
A tapping faint, yet persistent,
Ever there, yet slipping further from me.

"'Tis some crow," I whispered, "tapping at the emptiness I roam—
Only this and nothing more."

Ah, distinctly I remember, it was in a hollow December,
And each dying leaf and stagnant canal filled me with dread;

So that now, to still my weary heart, I paused,
Peering at the littered riverbed,
"Only this and nothing more."

The raven appeared, once proud, now weary,
Feathers darkened with soot, eyes dulled by neglect.
It had perched on ancient branches long dead,
Its voice now rasping, carrying the weight of many lost
seasons.

"Tell me," I murmured, "what fate awaits the world we
tread?"
Its beak opened once, then twice, and it rasped—
"Nevermore... Nevermore."

And in that instant, I understood:
Not only had the Earth been abandoned,
But the raven too had changed,
Its vigilance dulled by the relentless march of neglect,
Its song shortened, its patience spent,
No time to mourn what humanity discarded.

"Prophet," I cried, "shadow of wisdom, shadow of
sorrow!
Shall the rivers cleanse themselves? Shall the forests
return?"
It blinked, silent beyond the words,

And flapped away, wings dragging, leaving only
emptiness.

I was alone, the streets silent but for the wind,
The rivers still black, the air thick with apathy,
And the raven, once a messenger, now a wanderer like
me,
Had vanished into a sky too choked to hear.

And there, in the dim glow of poisoned lamps, I realized:
Loneliness is not only human—
It pervades the world, the creatures we once called
guardians,
And the Earth itself, neglected, waits for no one.

The moral lingered, sharp as winter's breath:
In our abandonment of nature, we abandon ourselves.
Even the watchers grow weary, and the songs die.
All that remains is silence,
And the echo of a Nevermore that no one heeds.

17. LAUGHTER IN THE SHADOWS: "GRAVELOCK"

Gravelock breathes in smoke and hunger,
its veins clogged with apathy, its towers cracked.
Darkness does not creep here—it thrives,
fed by ignorance, poverty, and fear.

He walks, painted grin wide,
eyes like fractured lanterns in the neon fog,
a maestro of ruin,
while the city's strings tremble under hands too weak to
hold them.

Even the mayor—a figure meant to guide—
sits in a gilded office, hands tied by debts and
compromises.
Dependence on oligarchs, unions, and empty promises
makes him fragile, a puppet of circumstance.
He calls the police, issues decrees—

but every command fades like mist into Gravelock's
smog.

Power weighs heavy,
Hands bound by fear and shadow,
Mayor whispers, lost.

No need for force; the Joker does not create chaos—
humans are already fractured, their rage, envy, and
despair
ready ammunition.
Even the city's guardians are compromised,
their principles drowned in bribes, ambition, and fear.

The Joker laughs, effortless,
a shadow dancing atop poisoned rivers and littered
streets.
He whispers into alleys:
"I do not make them broken. I only show you what is
already there."

Ash and grime converge,
Gravelock trembles under dusk,
Darkness claims its throne.

Schools lie empty; minds starve.
Hunger gnaws bones,

and knowledge does not feed the soul.
Every alley, every street corner,
is already a theatre for despair.

Even the Batman—a shadow in leather—
twists in moral decay,
a guardian blinded by ambition and fear.
Justice is a memory,
and in its place, only negotiation of shadows.

He dances across rooftops,
a marionette of carnage,
strings pulled by the hollow need
to see the world unravel.

Moon over Gravelock,
Silver grin splits the darkness,
Fools stumble, hearts crack.

The mayor trembles behind glass walls,
watching chaos spiral, powerless.
Every call, every order,
every plea for intervention
meets only bureaucracy, fear, and human weakness.
Dependence is his chain; helplessness his crown.

Rust and rot scent the air,

and somewhere, industrial hums become a hymn.
The laughter—high-pitched, bitter, and bright—
splits concrete like a blade.

He whispers in the ears of the night:
"Madness isn't a curse, it's a symphony—
a riff through the veins of the broken."

Steel drums hammer below,
trains groaning like beasts of burden,
and every shadow bends to his will.

Crowd melts into fog,
Gravelock exhales shattered glass,
Night owns every scream.

The city knows him, yet does not name him,
a wraith in painted skin,
an echo of chaos in leather and grime,
the pulse of disorder incarnate.

He disappears into the neon mist,
leaving Gravelock shaking,
its heart stuttering in discordant rhythm,
its soul screaming in minor chords.

Ash and smoke curl through alleys,

and yet, somewhere beneath the ruin,
a pulse—small, stubborn—remains.

"Despair is the city's breath,
but even in its smoke, sparks insist on dancing."

The Joker tilts his head,
watching humans stumble over their own darkness.
He laughs—not cruelly, but as one noting inevitability:
"The chaos was always written,
yet the next note may still surprise the orchestra."

Inside every chest,
The shadow laughs first, unseen,
I only join in.

Gravelock groans, yet its heart still beats,
a rhythm uneven, jagged, and alive.

"We are fractured yet not finished.
Even the shadows fear what light may remember."

The night tightens around rooftops,
rivers, alleys, and towers.
Though the darkness is thick,
and human frailty has ruled far too long,
somewhere—quiet, defiant—hope scratches,

waiting for the hand willing to shape it.

"The city will break, the city will bend,
but it will never wholly yield its breath."

Gravelock waits.
We wait.
The tension hums in the alleys,
a living reminder: despair is here,
but the next heartbeat may still rise.

18. FRIED FRITTERS BONDAGE

Once his stall was a carnival flame,
Where spices danced, and tongues sang his name.
Chef Lee, the master of street delight,
Whose ladle knew rhythm, whose curry took flight.

Butter hissed, oil gleamed gold,
Stories in steam, flavours bold.
Crowds once swarmed his glowing stand,
Coins clinked sweetly in his hand.

Chutneys, chutneys, and fiery hues,
Paneer tikka, noodles, and dumplings too.
Saffron and chili, basil and lime,
Every dish a melody, every bite a rhyme.

But time turned cold — the apps took flight,
The crowd moved on to screens and bytes.

New stalls rose with neon glare,
Copying scents that once bloomed there.

He stood alone one silent eve,
Counting losses he couldn't weave.
A few fried fritters, limp and done,
His empire fading, one by one.

"Maybe it's over," he whispered slow,
As stray dogs circled, tails hung low.
Then came a girl, eyes wide and thin,
A ten-rupee note clutched tight to her skin.

"Uncle," she asked, "just one plate please?"
Her voice was softer than a breeze.
He looked at the sign — it said twenty a plate,
But mercy can't measure by market rate.

He fried them fresh, crisp and warm,
The oil sang like an old charm.
She ate in joy, her hunger fed,
A sparkle of life where hope had fled.

And then he paused, a final plate to make,
Golden fritters for the night's last sake.
He seasoned each with care and grace,
Dreaming of tomorrow, a brand-new space.

That smile — it broke his binding chain,
Of loss, of doubt, of lingering pain.
He lit his stove with a brighter start,
Not from profit — but from heart.

For life, he learned, will always blend,
Surprise in corners, lessons at end.
Even cold fritters can feed the soul —
And sometimes, losing makes you whole.

19. THE GEOGRAPHY OF HER CAUTION

"अभयम् सर्वभूतेभ्यः"

Abhayam Sarvabhūtebhyaḥ
— Let there be fearlessness among all beings

She walks through the city like a whisper —
eyes alert, keys in hand,
her heartbeat syncing with the streetlights.
Every lane has a history,
every silence a map she knows too well.

She memorizes shadows —
the ones that follow too close,
the ones that ask without words.

Her courage is quiet,
but it burns — steady, unyielding —
like a diya refusing to drown in wind.

In the office of polished voices and polite restraint,
she balances her tone like fine glass.
A comment lands too soft to confront,
too sharp to ignore.
She smiles — not out of ease,
but because stillness can be safer than truth.

On the way home,
her phone glows like a talisman,
numbers ready —
because the world calls this precaution,
not paranoia.

Yet within her, another map unfolds —
not of fear, but defiance.
The map of Abhaya,
etched in generations who learned
to walk through danger
and still carry grace.

She remembers her mother's words —
"Be alert, not afraid."
and her grandmother's silence —

that ancient armor of endurance.

So she walks on —
through alleys of judgement,
through corridors of unwanted nearness,
through homes that sometimes forget
what safety should mean.

Each step a small rebellion,
each breath a quiet hymn
to the goddess she hides within.

And when dawn rises,
her shadow stretches longer than fear itself —
a geography rewritten,
by the woman who refused to walk unseen.

20. WHEN THE SKY KNELT

— A Parable of Sin, Storm, and Redemption

The rooster calls, the prayer begins,
Before the sun forgives the sins.
Women draw rangolis by the gate,
Each line a promise, each fear innate.

Cows are fed with whispered hymns,
The priest appears — gold on his limbs.
His beads are new, his words rehearsed,
He sells salvation, quenches thirst.

He blesses fields for a sack of grain,
Writes charms for luck, or cure for pain.
Collects the mangoes, the goat, the rice,
And calls it "god's own sacrifice."

By noon he sits beneath the neem,
Counting coins in the incense stream.
A widow waits with folded hands,
He asks for "faith" — she understands.

At dusk he walks the temple round,
Mock virtue in his voice profound.
He warns the young to curb desire,
Then meets his lover behind the pyre.

He drinks the milk before it's blessed,
Wears devotion like a borrowed vest.
Tells stories of heaven, of sin, of hell —
But owns the keys to the temple bell.

Then one fine day — the sky forgot itself.
The wind arrived like a long-lost debt,
Not roaring, but whispering, sly and deep —
It peeled the prayers the walls had kept.

The clouds did not thunder, they sneered instead,
Lightning walked barefoot through the shed.
Tulsi leaves turned black with shame,
The idols blinked — as if they knew his name.

The temple spire cracked like bone,
Ash rained where camphor had shone.

The priest ran out, clutching his beads,
But the storm recited his hidden deeds.

Water washed the sacred dyes,
Rangolis bled into the skies.
The village watched in silent awe —
Faith had teeth, and justice raw.

They searched the fields, the sacred pond,
Each prayer now a desperate bond.
His footprints ended by the stream,
Where smoke met dawn in a quiet dream.

Some thought he fled, his gold unspent,
Some swore the heavens took his scent.
Some thought he died — a sinner slain,
Some thought his guilt had turned to rain.

Years rolled on — the fields grew green,
The scars of the storm were seldom seen.
Children laughed where idols fell,
The past became a tale to tell.

Then one dawn — a tremor, a sign,
A saffron figure crossed the line.
Older, frailer, softer eyes,
Like dusk that still remembers skies.

He spoke with truth, not threats or charms,
He healed with words, not folded arms.
He built no walls, he asked no fee,
He taught that god begins in "we."

The village changed — the air grew mild,
Each elder smiled, each child beguiled.
The man who once had sinned so deep,
Had found his faith where guilt would sleep.

And one calm day, his breath grew still,
A soft wind sighed across the hill.
No gold, no sin, no fear to weigh —
Just folded palms and humble clay.

But that night came the storm once more,
Not fierce — but kind, from shore to shore.
The thunder bowed, the clouds stood still,
As if the heavens bent their will.

Raindrops fell like tears of light,
Blessing earth through endless night.
And dawn arose — serene, forgiving —
Proof that grace still walks the living.

The neem tree swayed, its roots made sound,

As if the sky had kissed the ground.
Yet whispers rose through village lanes —
Had he returned in flesh, or only in God's own veins?

Some said he had already died,
And God had lent him life, supplied,
A second chance to cleanse the past,
A soul reborn — meant to last.

And in that quiet, none could tell,
Where God ends, or man begins to dwell.
Faith lingered on, both awed and free —
For some things are only God's decree.

21. THE LAST POEM- "শেষের কবিতা"

We met where the sky touched the hills.
Words weren't needed; silence spoke.

Nothing belonged to us—not the future,
not even this moment fully.
We understood that love doesn't need to last
to be true.

It came lightly, like mist,
and left the same way—
without breaking, without noise.

No goodbyes. No grief.
Only the calm that follows
when two people know
that some things are complete
because they end.

The last poem is not written.
It exists in the space between us,
in the quiet that remains.